SISTER JANE

THE HIDDEN JOY

Edited by Dorothy Sutherland

Foreword by
Bishop Robert Runcie

SLG PRESS
Convent of the Incarnation
Fairacres Oxford

ISBN 0 7283 0148 2
ISSN 0307-1405

Printed by Will Print, Oxford, England

ACKNOWLEDGEMENT

The cover photograph is reproduced
by kind permission of Leslie Everhart.

Contents

FOREWORD

ALL OF US WHO love Fairacres and owe it so much will rejoice in the appearance of these meditations in manageable form. They are entirely free of those egoisms and anecdotes which help most of us to catch our readers' attention. They are not autobiography, but they ring so true that those of us who know Jane will hear her voice in every line.

Sometimes she is on her best behaviour. We sense the cost and agony of getting an important point right. They are not always 'lightning meditations'. She can speak 'out of the depths'. At other times they flow easily with the spontaneity and fun that finds in Siamese cats a Christmas message, or asks us to attend to the clown. 'Humour is near to holiness and love to laughter'. They puncture our self-importance.

Scripture, Liturgy and Rule shape her mind but never constrict it. She is gloriously, dangerously, open to other faiths and can be surprisingly sharp on those of us who don't live up to the implications of our own. At the heart of things there is waiting, silence and wonder. 'Yearning', says St Augustine, 'makes the heart deep.'

She is never afraid to fall back on common sense, and there is a streak of natural scepticism in her character which make her words of faith and fortitude still accessible to those who find it hard to believe. Above all, she reminds us that religion must never be a kind of defensive shell to protect ourselves against insecurity, other people and loss. Only when we give ourselves to the God who is outside ourselves can we know the freedom and life that has no end.

We should not be ashamed to say that these pieces of Jane are very much of the family; but we are a wide enough circle. They

warn us gently, amusingly, feelingly, just occasionally frustrat-
ingly, that every day we are faced with the choice between true
and false religion.

It was said of Edward King when he was Principal of
Cuddesdon, 'About the self discipline there could be no doubt.
But what was evident was the humanity, the breadth, the
naturalness. They found in him no tension, no pose, no tautness
that he could not relax. He was one of those rare spirits in
whom Grace seemed natural.' I am one of those who can say
that no church community has inspired me by those qualities
more than the Sisters of the Love of God. Perhaps Jane will
allow me to say that she has articulated that spirit both in her
listening leadership and in these treasured pages.

EDITOR'S PREFACE

THE SELECTIONS in this little book trace highlights of Sister Jane's understanding of the opportunities and obligations of total commitment to God—not merely as translated by the lives of the Sisters in a contemplative community, but as a way of life for all of us. They were published originally in the *Fairacres Chronicle*, hidden, appropriately enough, amidst the 'Community Notes' of each issue, the lead article traditionally contributed by the presiding Reverend Mother of the Sisters of the Love of God. Sister Jane, whose life in the Community spans almost forty years, was elected Mother in 1973 and served until 1988.

I first met Sister Jane in 1980 while visiting Fairacres for a fortnight, and during the intervening years came to know her wisdom and practical theology more intimately by following her editorial comments on Community life in the *Chronicle*. After she retired I found myself returning to the Notes and marking large chunks and small bits as gems of spirituality I wanted to preserve. I became curious about what she had been saying earlier in her tenure and had the good fortune to be provided with back copies of some twenty issues I had missed—covering in all forty-five *Chronicles* published during her term of office.

As I began to put her writings together, I became convinced that others searching to enrich their spiritual life and to deepen their faith could find encouragement and comfort in Sister Jane's teachings as I had. Whether she is writing about living or dying, harmony or violence, temptation or courage, caring or diffidence, all her teaching reveals her total commitment, her abiding love for God, and her unconditional hope for us, his human creatures, warts and tipped haloes notwithstanding.

It is tempting to call *The Hidden Joy* a collection of meditations on the contemplative life. But it is much more than that. It is, rather, a contemplative meditation on LIFE itself—not just life as it is lived under the Rule and disciplines of a religious order, but within the guidelines of the Christian faith so many of us claim but cannot always apply to the contradictions, the confusions, the competitiveness, and controversies of these end-of-century years.

In 1974, Sister Jane's first Christmas as Reverend Mother,

3

she wrote 'A Christmas Message' which was published along-side but not as part of the Community Notes. I read it not just as her lifelong dedication to the mystery of the Incarnation, but also as a testament to her faith. It expresses her love of God in the living Christ, in the Alpha and Omega of his birth and death for our reconciliation and our final redemption.

I have somewhat condensed this essay and have divided it into two parts to serve as Prologue and Epilogue, her own words leading us into and through this sampling of her spirituality. For in her thinking Christmas is not a one-day celebration each year, but the celebration of God in our lives every day.

She writes that Christ is born in each of us over and over again so that in our turn we may let his light shine out upon the world, transforming in our own small way its ordinary dailyness into his extraordinary beauty. And she urges us to offer to God our consciousness, our full selves, aware that although as human beings we are culpable of acts of monstrous evil, we are also capable of unselfish heroism on an even larger scale, affirming God in the midst of it all.

The SLG Rule addresses this God-centredness in simple but profound words, that when 'the whole being is set on God, the hidden joy which is beyond all natural attainment will be found'. Perhaps this anthology of Sister Jane's own centring may inspire all of us to find him in the very heart of all our hunger and hope. For, as St Augustine wrote, 'My life shall be a real life, being wholly full of Thee.'

DOROTHY SUTHERLAND
Arlington, Virginia
July 1994

PROLOGUE

'In the beginning was the Word...'

WHAT is certain about the 'message of Christmas' is that it is not one of soothing reassurance and cosy sentimentality. It tells of 'the things that cannot be and that are', something stupendous, too good to be true: but also

> '... this birth was
> Hard and bitter agony for us,
> like Death, our Death ...'

as T.S. Eliot writes of the Nativity in *The Journey of the Magi*. It is something which shatters our safe piety and challenges us to accept total insecurity and to be divested of every certainty. 'Traditional' observance of Christmas, sacred as well as secular, can blind us to what the eternal fact of the Incarnation really means.

At Christmas we believe that God was made man: but there is a danger that we may formulate this 'revealed truth' in a mother-child-and-stable concept that is safely remote from our own immediate circumstances.

God shows his love for us by taking a vast risk, and each Christmas we are jolted into looking at it afresh. He 'empties himself' and put himself into our hands so that we can reject and refuse him, misunderstand and abuse him, manipulate and use him. Or we can try, by his grace, to respond with a love that does, however feebly, take its character from his.

If we pray sincerely to have the mind of Christ, we must be ready to live by such a love that 'in all things and above all things' goes out to God—not as we think or hope he may be, but as he knows he is: and that finds its justification and fulfillment not in any sense of certainty, but in the fact that it is called into being by his love for us.

When we are shattered by what seem shocking statements and questions from theologians, we can be thankful to be shaken out of complacency into a realization that if the Christian faith is what we profess to believe, it must be a living reality that affects us every minute of every day, resting not in 'the wisdom of men but in the power of God'.

The Incarnation is what it is, no matter what we say about it. Truth has nothing to fear, and we cannot hide behind what we should like it to be, from the impact of what it is. Often what we are really anxious about is the threatened loss of our own reliable supports and structures. If we can submit to exposure, insecurity, and living at risk, we shall at least begin to understand what St Paul speaks of as 'the mind of Christ' in writing to the Philippians of Jesus' self-emptying.

Here, surely, is a way of poverty demanded of all Christians, whatever our material circumstances, our way of life, and theories of spirituality. Certainly, we who live in community, find it harder to be detached about our plans and opinions than about the material things we used to own. And yet, to 'those who know that they are poor', Christ promises the Kingdom of Heaven.

If we have courage to admit the reality of our situation, that we can rely only on God, we are open to receive the glory which will shine into every corner of our lives and ourselves, showing up the shadows most starkly, but inflaming us with a delight in God that keeps our perspective right and helps us to accept and transcend our own and other people's shortcomings because the love of God is so much more important.

HIDDEN   JOY

When the whole being is set on God,
the hidden joy in him is found.

THE contemplative life is a hidden life whether it is lived in
a convent or in the privacy of one's own home or in the
seclusion of a hermitage. It is hidden within the secret heart of
each individual who seeks to draw close to God by prayer—by
contemplating the wonder of his Word and his work, and the
glory of his love and his creation.

The Community of the Sisters of the Love of God began in
hiddenness, in a small semi-detached house between the Cowley
and Iffley roads in Oxford, with the windows whitewashed so
that the would-be nuns should not be distracted from attention to
the interior life and the things of God by what was going on in
the world around them.

We, their successors, cannot be grateful enough for the whole-
hearted response to God made by our foundation members, and
those who guided them. It was their courage and faithful
perseverance which brought the SLG community into being and
established the basic principles of its existence.

Our vocation remains essentially what it was at the beginning,
although in some ways its basic concepts are experienced and
expressed differently because the community has evolved with
the society to which it belongs. So we have the opportunity,
indeed the obligation, to know and thoroughly explore for others
and for ourselves what it means for Christians today to 'seek
God only' and to 'come into the wilderness' for the sake of
Jesus Christ.

THE DAYS are long past when SLG was virtually sufficient unto
itself and we permitted like-minded people an association with
us which was primarily for their benefit. We now know very
well that we need the enrichment brought to us by our fellow-
pilgrims travelling the same Christian way and sharing our

special concern for reconciliation and a thoroughly incarnated spirituality.

Some of our closest friends have no specific SLG label. But all connected with us, who often have a lonely struggle in their particular situations, can at many levels inject reality into our praying care, ensuring that it does not become idealistic and abstract, while the established Community can provide solid evidence of continuity and corporate commitment for them.

In the unity of Christ's love for all of us, we need—and share—each other.

THE MONASTIC WAY of life may be seen to symbolize the foolishness and hope of the Christian life in general and the religious life in particular.

It is a Way that could be total nonsense; and many wise people, Christians and others, consider it a wicked denial of the opportunities and obligations given by a good God to his creatures.

Part of the price to be paid by those who live it is acceptance of the rub that their critics may be right. For we cannot claim smugly that our way of witnessing to the fact that 'the foolishness of God is wiser than men, and the weakness of God is stronger than men' is the best or only one. But while monasticism can never claim to have all the answers, it has stood through the centuries and still stands today as a witness to the fact that the quest for what Christianity calls 'the true riches' is infinitely worthwhile.

A community of Religious comes into being not primarily because its members have chosen to live together, but because each has responded to what he or she experiences as a personal call from God for a self-giving to him that will be expressed by living with this particular group of people in the way in which they are drawn to serve him.

Insofar as a Religious Community contains persons varying greatly in origin, social status, training, and tastes, it represents a cross-section of human society; and its responsibility to transcend differences to a degree beyond mutual toleration and peaceful co-existence is a solemn one. The radical realization of our baptismal promises in Religious Profession cannot increase our commitment to God, which is already total; but it does underline it by a conscious, responsible decision, made not out of duty or for pleasure, but to affirm the folly of faith.

At her Profession a sister asks, by the mercy of God, to take the risk of learning to live the incalculable consequences of dispossession and disengagement for the rest of her life.

The structured security of a community such as SLG is understandably envied by some who face the prospect of a lonely old age in an unfriendly society. But the life vows which we make, in the folly of reliance on God's faithfulness alone, and which bind us to live day by day with the same people, can sometimes be experienced as piercing nails, tolerable only in 'the power of his resurrection'.

OUR life in religion is an attempt to live the gospel life and to suffer the consequence. If we are trying really to live by love and not by the law—that is, in risk, exposure, and constant impingement upon each other—then it will indeed be only by the grace of God that we can stay 'nailed to the cross of our Order'.

We are not meant to be cosy. We may have material security which is denied to and envied by many. But if there is in our life to be a real witness to the coming of the Kingdom of God's love, it will be at the cost of intimate involvement with, and space-making for, totally differing and often opposing views and opinions—even about the response to God that the Community is called to make. We are committed to each other by solemn vows made before God, and we cannot live and let live, comfortably anonymous in a group of fifty or so, cultivating our own salvation.

Our part in the work of God's world is to experience and accept the price of proximity which is paid in the turmoil of international affairs as we know them to be. Although our own awareness may be primarily of the defeat of love, only by faithfully persevering and 'not leaving' shall we be a reminder to other Christians that the Kingdom of God is attainable.

ALL CHRISTIANS are committed to fellowship with Christ in the totality of human experience. We must inevitably expect at some point in our lives to know, however dimly, something of the nailedness of the Crucifixion: to be tempted to wriggle out of an intolerable situation, but instead to be held in to it, because that is where Christ is. Personal response to God is the only way of truth at such times. It may well involve refusal to be deflected by our own desires or those of other people around us, and to stay with Christ because we love him, and because staying is the only valid thing to do.

One of the functions of a Religious Community is to demonstrate by the way we live the basic requirement of all forms of Christian living. By living together a common life and trying to transcend differences through a common attention to God above all else, it is not surprising that we experience a microcosm of all the divisions of humanity. It is our allotted task to meet them and in our small sphere to try to resolve them. We do this, not by uniformity of behaviour but by a constant and costly acceptance of and respect for that which sometimes appears to be in radical opposition to our own profound convictions—without denying or abdicating them!

WILLIAM TEMPLE, when Archbishop of Canterbury, wrote in his *Readings in St John's Gospel* that when Jesus exhorts anyone: 'Believe in me', the sense is 'Put your whole trust in me'.

Such readiness to take the risk of handing ourselves over to God should surely be at the heart of our Christian response to him. We have no reason to think that this surrender will ensure that everything is 'all right' for us. Quite the reverse, as the lives and works of the saints testify. But if we are trying with our wills to put ourselves in his hands, we can know that in life and in death we are in the right place.

The ordered discipline of convent life, however, does not ensure plenty of time for reflection. There is always the temptation to evade the need simply to be alone and still before God so that we may face up to things as they are, and live out the consequences of totally offering ourselves to him.

It is not so much a question of clock time spent in silence and solitude as of an attitude of mind that gives priority to waiting on God only. We are all able to lock ourselves into solitude designed according to our own specifications, protected from intruders. But if we are truly trying to put God first, we shall gradually grow to find him, and trust him, in persons and things—but above them—and to find all persons and things in him.

IN THE RELIGIOUS LIFE, the contribution of those living as solitaries is of vital importance. These SLG Sisters are as much concerned with relationships, for good and ill, as those who experience them in communal living. The life of the whole Community in Christ can grow healthily only insofar as we are all ready to give to and receive from each other at every level.

There is great scope for trust, generosity, and adventurousness as we see that certain Sisters can and should do exceptional things on behalf of us all, as well as great scope for fidelity and perseverance. Basically, all of us remain within the framework of the consecrated way of life, nailed to the cross of our Order—which means being irrevocably committed to each other.

The solitary life is not something exclusive and elite, for the advanced saint or the way-out eccentric. It is, in fact, one aspect of the Christian way among others, a form of living that proclaims uncompromisingly the basic truth which we all acknowledge in theory—that it is what God does with our lives that matters, and not what we do with them.

At times it is tempting to want to 'get away from it all' and to 'contract out' of twentieth century living, even as we edge closer to the twenty-first. But there is no magic time machine to propel us into some personal and private Wonderland. And if there were such a place, we would soon tire of it with no one there but our dissatisfied selves—still victimized by the acute loneliness that prevails in these painful times.

Although we may find the witness of the solitary life an uncomfortable reminder that poverty of spirit must be an ever-present and constantly reviewed and renewed reality for Christians, called as we all are to total commitment in faith, the heart of God-giveness is not so much renunciation as it is affirmation.

LIVING TOGETHER closely, as we do, does not solve communication problems. We work and eat in silence, and there is no place like a silent community for generating misunderstanding and incomprehension.

Every reader of a written notice is likely to interpret it differently, and the chances are that the writer's intention will be missed by all. We know that the problem is not peculiar to SLG and we can live with it and laugh at ourselves. We are a small example of the basic incapacity of one human being really to understand another. But the truth of the Incarnation brings hope! For God has done for each of us what we cannot do for one another: he has got inside our skins.

THE EFFECT OF WORDS on their hearers and readers is not always directly related to the meaning they contain; and the deliberate or inadvertent misinterpretation of what is spoken and written by other people is one of the hazards of these hazardous times. The power of language consists in more than the factual accuracy—or otherwise—of what it conveys, because it affects the emotions as well as the intelligence, and communication operates at many levels, conscious and unconscious.

We can diminish a concept or an experience by trying to articulate what words cannot capture. Words can also be used in such a way as to evoke something beyond what is actually said. Obviously, literary skills can be misused and orators can wax eloquent in praise or blame of the same set of facts, so that the victims of verbal bombardment are left wondering what is the precise relationship of word and meaning ... Alice had the same problem when communicating with Humpty Dumpty!

OFTEN WE FAIL to hear each other because we are too afraid or preoccupied to listen openly: we fear the loss of something precious to ourselves or we are too reluctant to risk the impingement upon us of another self if it comes too close.

But no one, however locked in loneliness by some particular anguish of body, mind, or spirit, is separated from the God who died 'outside the gate' in the extremity of God-forsakenness, and by so doing took the whole of creation into his unbroken unity. Although we feel we cannot be heard when we say this to someone in need, any more than we can hear it ourselves when we would wish to do so, we can trust God to make it known in ways beyond our reach; and we can believe, affirm, and live by the great and saving truth that he is Man and gives meaning to our existence.

A community whose Christian commitment is expressed through the life and work of prayer can and must be exposed to experience in many ways and at all levels if it is to be safeguarded from the dangers of unreality and idealism. Putting ourselves into another person's situation is one way. What is certain is that we are all concerned with, and affected by, what happens to each one of us. We cannot bypass any aspect of our own human nature if, through Jesus, we are going to be wholly given to God. We must have the courage to face and love ourselves if we are really to love our neighbour; and unless we do that we cannot properly love God.

CHRISTIANS, in or outside the Religious Life, can all too easily become grim, tight-lipped practitioners of self-sacrifice. We concentrate far more on ourselves and the offering we heroically make than on God. If we really love him everything will be freely and gladly given, regardless of what we feel in terms of consolations or awareness of him. We can shrivel into empty shells if we allow ourselves to be enslaved by Duty, devoting ourselves entirely to the impossible task of trying to fulfil, to our own satisfaction, the exigencies of a particular role we may happen to occupy at any time.

SIMPLY TO tolerate other people's views on a 'live and let live' basis is not really to comply with what the scriptures tell us to do about seeking and finding the Kingdom of God.

'Have this mind among yourselves', says St Paul, 'which was in Christ Jesus', and he proceeds to expound the obedience of Christ which led him to his death and exaltation. If we remember that 'obey' is a word deriving from *audire*, 'to hear', we see that far more than submission and loss of self-will is involved in Christian obedience.

Jesus Christ is pre-eminently the one who, in his early life, 'heard' and responded to every situation he experienced. 'In him', says St Paul again, 'it is always yes'; for he has shown us how to respect all persons, giving them space to be and to assent to all circumstances in such a way as to transcend them without any attempt at manipulation.

Twenty-five years ago, Father Gilbert Shaw reminded the Community that our work is listening—taking the situation we are in and 'holding it in courage, not being beaten down by it'. Our work is 'standing', he said, 'holding things without being deflected by your own desires or the desires of other people. Then things work out'.

It would be well for all Christians to learn to listen in that way for the sort of deepening in prayer that could bring about in us a change of heart and even of mind. The penitential seasons throughout the Church year give us ready-made opportunities to practice self-denial and the discipline of more acute listening to God and to people. But we can approach true 'conversion of heart' in yet another way, redirecting our entire life to the will of God rather than by imposing conditions on ourselves, as we are inclined to do, just for a day or a season.

Bodily appetites, indeed, can be for many of us a cause of humiliation and discomfort. But perhaps acceptance of this mortification, of our helplessness and sense of failure, brings us nearer to God, for he is always to be found in the outcast, disreputable parts of ourselves as well as of our society.

Really to listen to the situation we are in means silencing the clamour which is perpetually going on in most of us, protesting that things ought not to be as they are, nor should I be the sort of person I am, and all in all 'it's not fair'. When we come to the point of recognizing and accepting the facts, we can look at them objectively and make a response that is courageous because it depends on God's strength making use of our weaknesses. It often happens that when we are 'beaten down by it' we are overcome not so much by the practical difficulties that surround us as by the inner fuss we are making about imagined impossibilities.

If by listening we can discover the reality of the circumstances we are coping with—be they permanent or temporary—we can move on to the next step: to hold things without being deflected by our own or other people's desires—in other words, to 'stay with it', and to find in it the joy of the heart's desiring.

WHY this waste? This ointment', says St Matthew's gospel, 'might have been sold for a large sum and given to the poor'. It is unlikely that the disciples expected an answer to their question: certainly not the one they were given. This is the sort of question that 'do-ers' of any religion or of none, in all good faith put to contemplatives, we women and men who shut ourselves up in monasteries and convents when we might be 'doing so much good' outside.

Those of us who are called to withdraw in a measure from worldly ways should use the opportunity thus given to see things in proportion, fully to appreciate and delight in all that is good and true and beautiful in life. What matters in our giving to God is not so much the 'how' but the 'why'. When the story of the woman with the precious ointment appears in St Luke's gospel, it is the occasion for setting forth Jesus' teaching on love: not just when we first make or consciously confirm our commitment to God, but continuously, all along the way, suffering through life the cost of loving and losing, and that restlessness of which St Augustine writes, until finally we awake, 'after God's likeness and are satisfied...'

We in community know well how much easier it is to be cumbered with spiritual serving than to sit at the Lord's feet and really hear him. His truth is perpetually offered to us in so many different ways not overtly religious at all. Let us all pray especially for each other and for ourselves that we may have the courage to stand still before truth and, consequently, to seek beyond our reach.

Contemplatives are called to offer their lives to God, not primarily in works, but in worship, simply after the manner of the woman with the jar of ointment, to give him the love he needs: The omnipotent God needing love? Surely we must find that living by love makes us less and less self-sufficient. So it is reasonable to think that the same is true in some way of God who loved us first and who teaches us that freedom, choice, and risk are intrinsic factors in the sacrificial, self-giving love he gives and requires.

WILDERNESS

KYRIE ELEISON

JESUS' temptation in the wilderness may be a familiar story, but we cannot return too often to the lessons for life to be learnt from it. If we are seriously intending to worship and serve the Lord our God and not the Prince of Darkness, we cannot take short-cuts.

There are far too many stones in the world and not enough bread; but we cannot remedy the situation except by a basic change of heart leading mankind to live by the Word of God. Nor can we pressurize people into believing what we think is best for them, which is what Jesus would have done if he had defied the law of gravity and miraculously survived. In fact, his time in the wilderness led ultimately to the Way of the Cross and Resurrection because only so could the redemption of free persons be accomplished.

God respects each one of us as a mystery and we must do the same.

JESUS WAS and is willing to suffer and absorb the consequences of sin and has permitted us the freedom to follow him if we choose: a choice that sometimes takes the form of whether we accept or resist circumstances and events which we cannot avoid. But we mistake and diminish the richness of the possibilities he offers if we think in terms of recovering some supposed harmony humanity once had and has lost.

We have arrived where we are, how we are; and from there we go on. We cannot 'unknow' what we know, or drop the many and varied convictions to which we are committed. Unity is something much more exciting than a bland submission or absence of disagreement.

We see, according to St Paul, only 'in a glass darkly'. When we are able to accept that, it can be quite a relief to stop trying vainly to grasp things in the round and so to exercise control over them. How often it happens that our actual experience of

people or events is very different from what we have antici-
pated. We can be agonizingly apprehensive or foolishly sanguine
beforehand, and then be surprised, pleasantly or unpleasantly.

But there is more than this where other people are concerned:
however we think of them in absence, their presence introduces
an element we cannot bargain for. We find that, for instance,
the fear or anger we have been harbouring, or our innate and
reprehensible suspicion of strangers melts away if something of
a smile comes into the situation.

We need to remember that Christ himself is in each of us.

THE BREAKING DOWN of barriers between Christians expressing
different aspects of life in the Body of Christ is a welcome
development in our times, for which there is evidence in many
quarters.

Fear of, and therefore antagonism towards, what is 'different'
is deeply rooted in our human nature. Rivalry is an integral part
of life in society, and the innocent competition of a baby show
at a village fête can foster the spirit of curious comparison
which, as we are taught by the story of Cain and Abel, leads us
to destroy each other.

Christianity, however, affirms that each human being is
unique, incomparable and of infinite worth. In the complexities
of life together some are more fitted than others to do certain
jobs, but each of us, whether or not we appear to have found
our niche in our particular sphere of life, is destined to love and
be loved by God and other people in some special way.

There is no experience of joy or sorrow, no anguish about
another's grief and our own helplessness to help, no sense of
utter estrangement from God himself in which God has not
reached that place before us, so as to be in it with us. That is
why 'conversion of heart' means, for everyone, simply being
willing to acknowledge before God the full extent that we can
see of who and what we are, and our readiness to offer him the
sum total. Only so can we bring to him for healing the passions

of human nature that divide families, societies and nations, and that seem likely to destroy the world.

'Continual conversion of heart for the sake of trust' is an ideal attainable only if the mind of Christ is in us: but surely we have to acknowledge it is God's purpose for the human race.

'Gather into one the children of God who are scattered abroad'. Every one of us must affirm this not just as a pious hope but as a necessity for survival. Nothing short of conversion of heart—and ultimately each one of us is responsible for that—can change the policies of nations, because these depend upon the dispositions of their individual members. And everyone is of equal value and influence in the eyes of God, whose kingdom comes in ways quite other than those of political machinations.

'WHEN WILL the world learn that a million men are of no more importance compared with one man?' asked Thoreau.

Every corn of wheat counts; and in our age of mass-production and mass-reaction it is necessary constantly to remember that there is hope for the reversal of the seemingly inexorable movement of the world to self-destruction.

That hope lies in the stand taken against world destruction by individual persons and groups who try, in many and diverse ways, to live for and by God's love and to be prepared to pay the price.

Human inhumanity and the problems posed by suffering and love are nothing new. Today, all over the world, we know the scale of atrocities almost as soon as they are committed. But the agony experienced by each individual concerned must be essentially the same as that of the victims of religious persecution or political violence in all epochs.

Every person can only die once, however horribly. The terrible threat of nuclear annihilation which we live with increases the extent but not the intensity of the suffering that has always been in the world.

Some, not all, of us may see our Christian and humanitarian

vocation in terms of joining organized protests against injustice and other forms of violence. What all of us can do to make these effective in the cause of right is to look into our hearts and try to open them in all their murkiness to the healing power of God, confident that he will accept, forgive and use us, whether or not we are able to see the results.

JOHN DONNE, nearly four centuries ago, in his poem 'Satyr III', wrote:

'To stand inquiring right, is not to stray;
To sleepe, or runne wrong, is. On a huge hill,
Cragged and steep, Truth stands, and hee that will
Reach her, about must, about about must goe.'

It is becoming increasingly clear that unless we take seriously the message of these lines, the human race is in danger of destroying itself. We must surely recognize that no single person can rightly claim to be able to apprehend the 'whole' truth even if they believe it to be contained in their particular revealed religion.

As Christians knowing Truth as a Person, we realize that 'reaching her' involves an infinite journey into the infinite God. Nevertheless, he is our companion on the way as are also the myriad other mortals, past, present, and future, going 'about and about, up the huge hill' like ourselves, and catching all the time different facets from different angles of the one Truth.

We need always to remember and actually to affirm 'Truth's huge hill' and our partial view of her. We cannot ever know any situation in its totality. But however devastatingly dark things may seem to be, we can affirm that the love of God encompasses the whole of history in the Passion and Resurrection of Christ.

'I will lift up mine eyes unto the hills,
from whence cometh my help.' Ps. 121

IN this mad world we hear daily of massacres, assassinations and terrorism on the one hand—not to mention the soul-and-body-destroying conditions of some people's lives—and, on the other hand, we go to amazing (sometimes almost obscene) lengths to prolong existence where it seems inappropriate and even undesirable.

Because we know immediately and in great detail the worst that is happening everywhere, it is natural that we should be tempted to despair of the present and the future. The Christian hope, however, is something more than that God will intervene to put things right in a way recognizable to us.

The majority of the world's inhabitants would probably subscribe to the injunction 'thou shalt not kill', and would hold that life is to be preserved and enhanced. But the greatest evils are the destructive violence that motivates acts of annihilation; the indifference of some that causes others to despair; the fear and possessiveness that prompt characteristics of which we are all, probably, guilty in some measure. However, 'living' as we know it, even at its most pleasant and privileged, leaves much to be desired.

The present breakdown of law and order in sections of British society means that we are having to experience at close quarters what we have hitherto read, heard about, and viewed as foreign news. It is obvious that we are all caught up in global complexities from which there seems no way out, and in which there are no 'goodies' and 'baddies' and no easy answers.

We cannot escape facing squarely the impossibilities of the present and submitting to their impingement upon us at a personal level. The distress and perplexity of nations is always being echoed in the personal situations of individuals; and no human being can be protected by ignorance or indifference from the suffering involved in being human.

If, in personal and private as well as in public and international circumstances we can, as it were, 'look over the head' of any particular impasse, head-on collision or confrontation, we can glimpse the possibility of an expanded vision of truth where what we know as negative, opposing tensions can be held together constructively.

WE INCH TOWARD this if we are aware of and positively affirm all that is good in life as we know it and refuse to be downed by what we read in the papers or see and hear in news bulletins.

There is so much to be thankful for in creation and in all that is being done by so many to try to preserve and protect it, and to work for social and political justice. But the real slog for each one of us is the turning of our own hard heart towards the dangers of being possessed by God, away from the seeming safety of self-made security.

This means being open to the unexpected. Automatically, we tend to assume that we cannot tolerate or be tolerated until we conform to each others' expectations. But if we risk living together or working together because of a common commitment to an ideal (or to a Person), we discover the probability of accepting and being accepted by each other as we are.

Brave women and men, within the Church and beyond it, work tirelessly for the welfare of the immigrants and under-privileged citizens in Britain and endeavour to awaken our apathetic society to the iniquities of class divisions, inequalities of opportunity, and persecution of minorities, overt or implicit, but still the words of the Prophet Isaiah remain true:

'And he looked for justice, but behold bloodshed;
for righteousness, but behold a cry...'

THE point of going into the wilderness is to leave behind what is safe and known, to turn one's back on what is past. 'Because I do not hope to turn again', is a phrase which T.S. Eliot uses repetitively in his poem *Ash Wednesday*, in which an exile laments failure, and regrets time and events lost or wasted:

> '...Because I do not hope to turn again
> Let these words answer
> For what is done, not to be done again
> May the judgement not be too heavy upon us...'

and petitions God to 'teach us to care and not to care; teach us to sit still...'

Contrition means recognition—often, as in the case of the Prodigal Son, through painful failure—of what has been wrong, and readiness through love, not self-interest, to admit it, to ask pardon and to take the consequences. The Prodigal can have enjoyed the feast and the fatted calf only if he cheerfully accepted the humiliation of looking a fool himself, and generously entered into his father's joy. It is good to suppose that he did, for his father's sake.

Penitence is something completely other than the guilt or remorse which are self-regarding sicknesses afflicting most of us to some extent, and which must be recognized as such and treated accordingly.

IN GENESIS 4:7 at least three modern versions of the Bible describe sin as an animal crouching at the door to overpower Cain who must resist it. This graphic description of sin as an objective force is something foreign to much contemporary thinking, but it can be helpful to an understanding of penitence, which has always been seen as an important part of prayer, and particularly as having an intercessory force.

Whether or not we can accept belief in a personal devil, to acknowledge that sin is something external and objective trying to impair our response to God, gives grounds for hope that we can, with God's help, get away from and dismiss evil in a way that we cannot if it is wholly internal and subjective, explicable by our personality disorders, heredity, or our environment.

One of the profound insights in the Genesis stories is the central place given to self-justification, which is so strong an instinct in us all. It is surely a common experience to have a quite irrational reluctance to acknowledge our culpability to God or a fellow human being: and yet when we can, we find how easy it is to do. 'Have mercy upon me, O God, after thy great goodness: according to the multitude of thy mercies, do away mine offences'.

THE PENITENTIAL PSALM 51 has a central place in the Church's liturgical worship, and while each of us can rightly apply all it says to ourselves personally, it can and should be used as an expression of solidarity with the whole sinful world. For this to be more than a pious thought we must claim and know our own particular involvement, accepting that we cannot escape complicity in responsibility for the whole world's being as it is.

Evil is contagious. It can be contained and defeated, as Dr C.B. Caird writes in his commentary on the Beatitudes, 'only when hatred, insult, and injury are absorbed and neutralized' by love, nor can we pursue our own salvation by trying to evade it.

Thanks to our belief that 'God is as he is in Jesus', we know that his love does absorb evil, and that we can ourselves be enabled to extend to others and to receive from them forgiveness in this way.

Because we know that God's love for and forgiveness of each one of us is total and unconditional, we can have hope.

ACH year the Church's liturgical cycle gives us new opportunity to go out into the wilderness from the point where we are now. Perhaps it will mean literally creating more silence and solitude in our lives. Perhaps it will not be possible to do this outwardly, so that we must make an effort and look inside at what has to be faced.

In any case, an experience of going into the wilderness means facing fear. Ascetic disciplines are not to be limited to nor despised as part of Lenten observance, but they must always lead to greater dependence on God. Watching and fasting demonstrate a mild defiance of natural rhythms in order to emphasize the prior importance of God's dimension. These are exercises we need to weave into our quiet times of self-examination periodically, not simply being reserved for the prescribed times designated in the liturgy.

Learning to accept the frustration of our own non-activity helps us to become aware of God's action in us. Above all, if we can still our restless memories and imaginations we shall discover and release the prayer that God himself is making within us, and has been making ceaselessly throughout our lives.

Often God's voice is overlaid by layers of our emotional reactions or occupational concerns when we do find time for contemplation of—or within—our own special wilderness.

If our scale of values is right, surely God's prayer in us should be the steady beat, the very heart-beat continuing through all aspects of our Being.

'Create in me a clean heart, O God,
and renew a right spirit within me...' Ps. 51

PRAYER

'Lord, teach us to pray'

A FORMER Bishop of Oxford once said that 'the praying life tends to become narrow unless all the time it is refreshed and enriched by the needs of the whole world.' In our individual Christian lives, this means that whatever the shape of our commitment, our prayers must continually be expressed in the context of the here and now, whenever and wherever that may be. Prayer needs to be made incarnate in and for the world today.

Often we trivialize the tremendous doctrine of the Incarnation by clinging to the misplaced assumption that, because God's Son became Man and dwells among us, everything will be 'all right' —meaning all right in terms that we can recognize. Then, when manifestly all is *not* right, our faith founders and we ask ourselves 'Why pray?'

Ever since Hiroshima we have lived with the possibility, expressed by Vatican II, that 'in spite of all the wonders of modern science, humanity ... may be brought to the point that the only peace it will know will be the dread peace of death.'

Modern life is filled with unresolved tensions. As Rowan Williams emphasized in one of a series of talks, 'the clash of apparent absolutes, the puzzlement and darkness, failure, death—all are seen as the only mode of created existence possible, and the only vehicle of salvation possible.' What a dismal vision!

As we pray, let us remind ourselves that prayer is not a last ditch hope when all else fails. Prayer is, rather, a universal force for mustering the Light of Christ to quell the powers of darkness around the world.

THE WORLD is unsafe and is being rapidly despoiled, but it is beautiful and well worth living in. However inhumanly we behave towards each other as individuals or as societies, we must believe that because God has taken our humanity upon himself, 'once and for all' no one of us is ultimately unredeemable.

Praying about all this means not simply washing our hands of the problems and passing it on to God as 'too difficult', but living with the consequences of confusion and contradiction, those within ourselves as well as amongst ourselves, and continuing to affirm God in the midst of it all.

A VIVID ACCOUNT in the Book of Judges tells of the angel of the Lord appearing to Gideon and saying to him 'The Lord is with you, you mighty man of valour'. And Gideon said to him, 'Pray, sir, if the Lord is with us, why then has all this befallen us?'

We pray and expect—and it natural to do so—that God's favour and presence will be indicated by things 'going right' for us: but in fact, how few of us can be sure that prayer is heard and answered (although it is, even though we cannot easily count the ways)? How do we get what we want or want what we get (and even if we do, the passage of time ensures that we cannot keep it)?

Health and fullness of life tend eventually to deterioration and decay, and many lives and personalities seem to have not even a chance of fulfilment. But Christian teaching is that 'we do not lose heart. Though our outer nature is wasting away, our inner nature is being renewed every day' (2 Cor. 4:16). Renewal—that is one of the reasons why we pray. Through the example of the Cross we know that true life does indeed continue through death for the preservation of every link of love.

DOM André Louf, in his book, *Teach Us to Pray*, makes the point that we tend to think of the will of God—especially in the religious life when it is mediated through a superior—as something pre-determined, opposed inevitably to our own wishes and judgement, which we have to 'obey', willy-nilly. He shows that, on the contrary, the derivation of the biblical word for 'will' has to do with caring, love, desire: and that Jesus in his agony, passion, and death transformed the refusal of the humanity he had assumed into assent in the dimension of God's love.

However we pray, the ways in which God draws each one of us are 'as varied as the heart of man': we pray by the Holy Spirit, in and through Christ the Word of God, and we find inspiration in the words of Scripture.

Father Gilbert Shaw used to remind that we can never have enough of Scripture and that nothing can take the place of the holy books through which God speaks to us. Perhaps we need to appreciate more deeply and make better use of the opportunities we have, whatever our way of life, to meet the Word of God in Scripture as well as in the Sacraments.

IN THE LIFE of prayer, intercession is for many of us and for other Christians the purpose of the whole of life. No human being can escape the fact that we are all inextricably involved with our fellows—and with the whole of creation. We are not only affected by each other's actions but share the same basic human nature and cannot avoid taking account of each other, simply because we have to inhabit the same globe.

Intercession is the basis of any attempt to find a *modus vivendi* and to look beyond the confrontation of conflicting interests to convergence in a common good.

Because we cannot fail to impinge upon and to be impinged upon by each other, and to recognize that we cannot escape the common lot of humanity, everyone's life is, insofar as it manifests care and concern at all, a kind of intercession. Any who practise intercessory prayer in this way, however, would disclaim any intention of or desire for prayer in the generally accepted understanding of the word. On the other hand, there are many who have such a desire but who feel that prayer is the business and prerogative of 'professional' spiritual persons; something esoteric beyond the reach of every woman and man.

PRAYER—which is really our most direct way of relating to God—so often comes to be regarded as 'something extra', something beyond or outside our usual daily occupations and preoccupations. But of course, it is as much an integral part of our existence as the breathing of which we are, generally speaking, equally unaware. We do need to ensure special times 'for God only'—for our sakes, not just for his—in order to establish the fact of his primary importance to us, and our desire to have him with us in everything we are or do. God will be with us whether we wish it or not, and it requires humility on our part to accept his knowledge about areas of ourselves and our activities which we would prefer to keep hidden. But here enter hope and love:

> 'A broken and contrite heart, O God,
> shalt thou not despise ...'

and if we bring that to him we know that we can go humbly and confidently with him into the future.

THE high altar of the Fairacres chapel is for many an outward sign of life's priorities, a sort of wicket gate into the looking-glass world of God's dimension, where the values and expectations we tend to take for granted are turned upside down.

The 'praying always' enjoined by St Paul, and practised by the Desert Fathers and others whom we regard as spiritual giants, is really simply a refusal to accept as ultimate and inevitable the various circumstances and situations in our lives that appear to be so. It is a constant endeavour to hold on to the fact that God's view of things is slanted differently from ours and to find our personal way of keeping constantly in touch with him. Some people find it possible to have a form of rhythm prayer going on all the time at the back of their minds; others use 'arrow prayers' periodically.

A helpful form of the 'rhythm prayer' is the Jesus Prayer which we inherited from the Orthodox tradition—'Lord Jesus Christ, Son of the living God, have mercy on me, a sinner ...' And any self-made ejaculation, for example the simple but fervent plea, 'Lord, help!' serves to shift our focus from ourselves onto God. It is so easy to want to make a mystique of prayer, a formula, something eloquent like the language of the King James Bible, or passionately poetic like St John of the Cross, or in the high realms of mysticism occupied by St Teresa of Avila. Actually, we can find appropriate and beautiful 'prayers' in a single line or couplet from most of the Psalms, and 'arrow' prayers in the Book of Common Prayer and the Alternative Services rites—the most obvious being 'Kyrie eleison' as petition, and 'Thanks be to God!' as an all-day way of acknowledging his action among us.

Each of us must find our own particular way of 'praying always' as our personal relationship with God develops.

'I will give thanks to thee, O God, with my whole heart because of your love and faithfulness ...' Ps. 138

EXPERIENCING reconciliation and unity in outward circumstances is only really fruitful if the inner conviction is shared, lived, and prayed with others—members of our local parish, families, friends, our Sisters in Religion. In SLG we learn more about this every year as we contemplate the lessons to be learnt from our patronal feasts.

The feast of the Transfiguration does not show, as is sometimes held, that the few—religious communities among them—pray on the mountain-top for and instead of those on the plain below.

On the contrary, the implication is that we are all to be with Jesus on plain and mountain. The clouded sense of loss, absence, and unknowing is as much prayer as are the moments of dazzling awareness.

JESUS spoke some very searching words about Truth: 'I am the Way, the Truth, and the Life ...' It seems to us wholly appropriate to think of truth in terms of personhood rather than being a matter of merely factual accuracy, or an abstract quality. We can accept, by this means, that it has a mysterious kind of Being which we can recognize and respond to but not define. We pray to God 'through Jesus Christ our Lord' whom we know as 'a Person' and who has told us that we 'know the Father' by way of knowing the Son.

In our prayer time, much of which needs to be listening, we receive the truth of God in such measure as we can, relating to him directly through Jesus and indirectly through all the ups and downs of daily life and prayer. He searches us out and knows us, and wants us to affirm him in all the really bad bits of ourselves and our experience, as well as in the times which we deem not so bad and therefore more presentable.

The human heart can never be converted by anything other than the free will of its owner; and unless and until we deliberately choose to turn to God and away from the gratification of ego needs as individuals—and from global destruction as nations—he will not, and cannot by his nature, make us do so. This is a fact of love which we have to believe and hold on to, part of the tension we must suffer, especially in our prayer life, without being able to resolve it.

Such readiness to know in ourselves the pain and bewilderment of the human condition is part of what constitutes prayer. We offer to God our consciousness, to bear the weight of personal awareness that as human beings we are capable of suicidal bomb attacks and massacres in churches—but also of acts of unselfish heroism on a large and small scale.

JESUS IS, has been, and always will be, humanly present with every being. We affirm this for others and for ourselves in our thought and prayer, certainly, but also in some measure practically, by learning to cherish each successive present moment as the meeting point of time and eternity where mortal and immortal converge.

In the Eucharist, we pray that proclamation of faith which tries to express the inexpressible:

'Christ has died; Christ is risen; Christ will come again.'

God was, is, and shall be; he transcends time yet he is of it and in it. It is he who turns our worldly values upside down and, in a climate of opinion where achievement and enjoyment are all-important, we do well to look closely at the element of holy folly.

As we begin to pray, we can ask God to remind us that he prays in us first. Only God can know the whole truth of any person or any circumstance. So things that appear to us as contradictions are, perhaps, contained and complementary in a dimension beyond our imagining. Although we cannot stretch our finite minds to understand this, we can try, in faith, to acknowledge it.

LOVING

'Love was his meaning'

WE cannot bypass any aspect of our human nature if, through Jesus, we are going to be wholly given to God. We must have the courage to face and love ourselves if we are really to love our neighbour; and unless we do that we cannot properly love God.

Love has been rightly called 'an outstripping of limits'. It cannot be grasping, possessive, or safe. It must always be ready to go with Jesus into the unexpected and unknown. This is the way, the only way, for all Christians.

Love means being alongside, in companionship; rejoicing with or suffering helplessly with—not instead of—the beloved, and delighting in the other as a person. This, surely, is something of what Jesus teaches about God's love for us, and about what ours can be, reciprocally, for him.

We do not find evidence, in Scripture or tradition, that acknowledgment of and response to God's love for us will shield us from pain and discomfort or ensure that 'all goes well' for us on our terms. On the contrary: Christian living is a matter of repeated dying, in one way or another, in order to be raised repeatedly by God into his dimension, until we finally know this as our homeland.

In the course of our Christian discipleship, most of us find that when we try, however fumblingly, to follow God's way he takes us at our word and one bottom or another falls out of our lives. We are left with a love which depends not on his doing for us what we had hoped and expected, but on the glimpse we have had of a Person who originally claimed our allegiance and retains it because of what we believe about him.

CHRISTIANITY does not pretend to offer a solution to the perennial problem of reconciling sin, evil, and pain with the concept of a loving Creator, Redeemer, and Sanctifier, but it does demonstrate the ultimate concern of a God of love for his universe.

God cares infinitely about each individual, and in these days of mass movements and collectivizations we do need constantly to remember to evaluate good and ill in terms of specific instances. Just as the suffering of one matters as much as that of millions, so one experience of goodness and beauty is of equal value in the opposite scale.

We cannot attempt to justify God's ways, or presume to think we know what he should do; but we can affirm our faith and hope and love by willingly 'keeping on keeping on' in the face of life's impasses and by being alert to delight in the evidences of God's love and care which are there for eyes that can see them. And we can try always to offer the whole gamut of human experience to God, trusting him to use us for his purposes, which are beyond our understanding.

TO RESPOND in faith and courage to what God asks of each of us is required of everyone who claims to be Christian. As Andrew Louth writes, 'truly to love means to be ready to receive...'

The virtue of giving is so much emphasized, however, that we easily forget the primary importance of being able to receive. It may be more blessed to give (and it certainly produces satisfaction and makes us feel happy) but in order to give to God and to each other the 'one thing necessary'—ourselves— we have to be ready to let go of a great deal of protective clutter at many levels. That is the only way we can be empty enough to receive the love and truth of God.

It is easy to think of God as the supreme giver: he gave his Son. But we also need to think of how much he received. He emptied himself in total poverty and accepted all the limitations of being human in a dependence that has much to teach us about the true meaning of poverty.

Christ's poverty meant that he was exposed to receive whatever came, good or bad, and while he was ready to take action if needed, this was always the fruit of his response to God in the present moment, never of a personal desire to control the situation.

IN *Four Quartets*, T.S. Eliot refers to the Incarnation as 'the hint half guessed, the gift half understood ...'

When we are confronted with the sacrificial, self-giving love that causes God to risk all for the sake of gaining all in terms of a free and loving response from his creatures, speculation and surmise lead only to wonder and to worship. Human love is seldom merely a neatly reciprocal matter of mutual exchange. It is a mystery which, diminished by attempts at definition, when received from one person we are, more often than not, enabled to give in our turn to another.

LOVING IS such a wide term that it can be emptied of practical application. A priest once told me that parishioners will act 'for the family' in blatantly selfish ways and see themselves as altruistic; and it is all too obvious how 'national' interests are currently fragmenting the world. We give lip service to such familiar commands as 'Love thy neighbour' but in our hearts may be uncertain what that really means. How often we hear it said that, 'Well, of course I need to love so-and-so, but need I also *like* him?

It seems to me that God wants us to do more about living together in mutual liking, rather than dismissing that affection as something given—or withheld—by nature, and being content to conclude that loving is all that matters.

A sister with whom I once spoke about loving vs. liking gave me a succinct answer from *Look Back with Love*, a book by Dodie Smith:

'True liking implies a reasoned judgement, and I have come to believe it is more important than loving: it wears better.'

Really to bother to know and understand another person will, with determination and goodwill, bring one eventually to discover that this is the stuff of which the Love of God is made. We can, alas, all too readily proclaim with Charlie Brown's friend Linus that we 'love mankind; it's human beings we can't stand.'

WHATEVER THE particular personal conditions of our life, we shall find in it achingly empty spaces. Even the closest companionship leaves gaps, and the God who made us for himself is not always there to fill them.

Christians can make sense of the loneliness which is for so many people something terrifying to be avoided at all costs. If we walk toward it, into the wilderness, our perspective alters and we discover new and unexpected richness in our situation when we can accept it as it is and stop regretting that it is not otherwise.

The spiritual wilderness does flower and is, as the early Fathers discovered the geographical desert to be, a lovable place if we are alert and expectant to search for and respond to all that is in it. All sorts of sudden delights will surprise us into wonder and loving worship.

There is no depth of degradation or alienation wherein Christ does not offer from alongside us the fellowship of love. God in Jesus has plumbed the worst that human beings can experience, even to the ultimate sense of alienation from God himself. But God raised Jesus from that worst and by so doing manifested the victory of love that he had been winning all his life. Here, surely, is something for us to grasp and affirm: God, partaking of human nature and subjected to its badness and goodness, which is still what it has always been, has made a statement about the ultimate defeat of hatred and evil. Love prevails.

FOLLOW ME! That is the whole of a Christian's duty, and 'that is the whole of a Christian's reward', wrote Archbishop William Temple.

The Church encourages us to think of following Jesus on his journey to Jerusalem, and as it reaches its climax, we enter with him into death and resurrection.

We think of ourselves as experiencing these mysteries, and indeed our life of discipleship is based on our belief that the purpose of existence is to do so. But we must never forget that we follow first and foremost a Person, and only consequently his way. Because that way leads us to be with him, we can and must lay hold upon the reality that he lives his life in and through each of us, here and now.

To follow Christ in love means not merely the observance of prohibitions and restrictions which we tend to associate with Duty, but a glorious expansion into increasing awareness of the wholeness of his dwelling within our lives.

We limit the majestic mystery of Redemption if we think too narrowly of Christ's obedience to the Father by enduring the Crucifixion and painful death. Rather, we should see in this great, living, ever-new event, the 'obedience' of God himself, being true to the nature of his love.

WE HAVE TO BE HUMBLE to admit that we cannot and do not need to understand the mind of God. What humanity has been and is still learning through the birth of Jesus nearly two thousand years ago is that we are invited, not compelled, to love God. He risks our refusal but never gives us up. If we struggle beyond our natural concepts of what constitutes happiness for humankind, in the midst of the anguished divisions and losses we experience, we will find assurance of eternal harmony.

We are, generally speaking, so much more informed and articulate than we used to be that we are often unaware of the many false assumptions we make about God and life. There is a very great deal that we do not and cannot know.

If only we were better able to abide in the present, we should find God's perfect rhythm at the heart of existence.

THE true value and purpose of birth, death, and life lie in a realm beyond the reach of our determining. It has been stressed by modern theologians of the Church both in East and West that the Incarnation is 'not an answer to sin: it is God's eternal longing to become man, and to make of every human a god out of grace.'

Because God fully shares our human living and enters into its risks, uncertainties, and tragedies, transcending them not by divine omnipotence but by sacrificial suffering love, we can have hope in the midst of despair, and we can trust through torment and disaster.

No one should minimize the solemnity, loneliness, and hard cost of death; but surely we cannot doubt that there is some element of continuity when a loved soul is taken by its 'Father for eternity' into the fuller realization of a fellowship glimpsed, perhaps unwittingly, during life on earth.

THE HEART AND essence of Christianity is this: the conviction that human experience is contained within a spiritual context.

Because God shares our life, we share his, and physical death is a question of change, not extinction. But this in no way minimizes the pain caused by parting from beloved persons or places; nor does conviction about spiritual togetherness alleviate the anguish of actual apartness.

To grieve realistically about the one is not to deny the other. Thoroughly to accept loss without trying selfishly to hold on to the departed can, in fact, lead the bereaved forward to a liberation and some comprehension of what is beyond. It is, however, easier to speculate about this in theory than to believe it in the midst of the experience.

Death belongs with time: it ends our portion of it. But death does not, cannot, erase the love that lived within the time of our lives, for love is greater than death and ascends with our souls into Life Eternal.

IN HIS BOOK, *Programs of the Brain*, Professor J. Z. Young writes: 'We shall not go far wrong if we keep respect for life as the central criterion by which every man's life can be judged'.

It is imperative to recognize and retain our human ignorance and powerlessness if we are truly to appreciate the dignity bestowed upon us by God's love and grace. That, in ourselves and in others, we ignore at our peril.

Respect for life diminishes appallingly as the end of this century approaches. More urgently than ever we need to affirm the message of the Incarnation, that human life is part of God's eternal life and that we can be fully alive in time only if we are conscious of the glory of his holiness penetrating, surrounding and transcending time. Let us hope that he will prepare us for the unforeseeable grace of abiding with him in Eternity.

DARKNESS AND LIGHT

'The light shines in the darkness
and the darkness has not overcome it...'

WILLIAM Temple, commenting on John 1:5 writes:

> 'Imagine yourself standing alone on some head-
> land on a dark night. At the foot of the headland
> is a lighthouse or beacon, not casting rays on
> every side, but throwing one bar of light through
> darkness ... The divine light shines through the
> darkness of the world, cleaving it, but neither
> dispelling it nor quenched by it.'

The conflict of light and darkness is basic in the mythology of
many creeds and cultures: almost instinctively we expect and
desire a conclusive outcome; and because 'Light' equals 'Right'
we assume that it will eliminate the darkness. But the message
of the Incarnation, the supreme saving action of God, is not that
he has mightily overcome by superior force all that opposes his
goodness and love; rather, that he has reversed our ideas of the
manifestation and exercise of power and challenges us to accept
the discomfort of sharing in the contest on his terms.

As we try to live by Christian values we have to accept that
light and darkness coexist in every sphere of life. We are constantly having to choose; and often the choice is between two
evils, or two options both of which are less than 'good'. Each
situation has to be met and judged on its own merits and very
seldom can we see immediately and clearly how to reject the
darkness and affirm the light.

Sometimes there is the opportunity to make a costly and
courageous stand for truth and righteousness, and we should be
just and generous in acknowledging the integrity of people who
do so, even when we do not agree with them. All too often it
seems that we are asked to stay with the perplexity and
ambiguity of unquenched light in undispelled darkness. In a grey

situation, it can happen that the only response is a grey one, and part of our prayer must be our willingness to accept the pain of compromise and helplessness that comes from our encounters with persons and circumstances as they actually are.

Jesus had a ruthless regard for reality, and went through life stripped of the protection of illusions. The man whom we meet in the Gospels is free from preconceptions and prejudice and, above all, from self-deception.

The knowledge we have of Jesus by faith demands of us conformity to his mind and outlook so that we can be pathfinders in the darkness, affirming that the light is there; and that in the midst of temporal life, which has in itself so much that is good and true and beautiful, there is a way into life eternal.

This knowledge enfolds its opposite, never denying it but asserting that those values are not ultimate. The final fulfillment and the 'answers' are beyond what our finite selves can grasp, in a place where, as Saint Augustine says, 'we shall rest, and we shall see; we shall see, and we shall love; we shall love, and we shall praise. Behold what shall be in the end, and shall not end.'

IN EVERY AREA of life there is a balance of change and permanence. Each season in nature, as well as in the Church's year, is new and old; different and the same. There are cycles in history and patterns in the universe; and in our own lives we sometimes experience a sense of 'having been there before' in place and time.

Perhaps it is not altogether unreasonable to think that when we come to physical death we shall find some element of familiarity, whether or not we have known God in terms of 'religion'. Apprehensions of truth and beauty in any form touch what we feel to be imperishable. It is hard to believe that in their deepest and dearest aspects human relationships do not endure beyond death.

S IAMESE CATS, I read recently, 'are greedy, demanding, jealous, and destructive', among other things, 'but they also have an unsurpassed depth of affection for the owner.'

These remarks may offend cat-lovers, among whom I am perhaps one of the most ardent. Still, I cannot resist finding a message here for Christians. Often we hear jibes that persons of other faiths (or of none) are much pleasanter in personality and more admirable in social concerns than we are. While we ruefully admit that such criticism may be justified, perhaps we can reckon to have something in common with Siamese cats.

The *Good News Bible* translates 2 Corinthians 1:21,22:

> It is God himself who makes us sure, together with you, of our life in union with Christ; it is God himself who has set us apart, who has placed his mark of ownership upon us and who has given us the Holy Spirit in our hearts as the guarantee of all that he has in store for us.

It is by the 'depth of affection for the owner' rather than by our moral rectitude or qualities of character that our allegiance to Christ is primarily tested and proved.

Most of us cannot assert that the majority of Christians lead Christ-like lives, but it is important that we see the business of our calling to be concerned principally with growing into love with God, rather than achieving results that merit commendation ... No harm in suggesting, however, that we might benefit by taking a lesson or two from the sociable, articulate—and friendly, though lap-sitting—tabby.

I EXPECT there are times when many of the baptized who take Christianity seriously wish that they need not do so; for believing that God is truly involved with mankind in the way shown by Jesus means that we are offered the opportunity to be truly involved in God's redemptive work. So we have the option of deciding whether or not to respond by accepting the consequences, and knowing also 'the fellowship of his sufferings'.

THROUGH   THE   YEAR

'Christ yesterday and today ...
all time belongs to him.'

THE COMING

THE POWER of the Lord's coming! That is the promise of the beautiful Advent responsory: 'I look from afar and behold! I see the power of God's Coming, and a cloud covering all the land. Go ye out to meet him and say, tell us if thou art he that shall reign over God's people, Israel.'

With Advent, the Church's year begins again. Although we know the course it will take, there remains always the element of mystery, an unknown something beyond our control and prediction, expressed liturgically in our prayer of hope and expectation.

Waiting, watching, and hoping are all key themes for the Advent season, and they can shape our attitude to life as a whole, beyond our immediate preparation for Christmas.

Because modern technology and the amazing recent developments of science indicate the possibility of our advancing indefinitely in understanding and control of life and environment, we risk losing that capacity to expect the unexpected which characterizes the humility essential for being fully human.

DURING ADVENT we wait and watch and hope for what has already happened, appeared, and been realized in the historical birth of Jesus Christ. But if we can enlarge our awareness we can become alert to what is continually new and surprising. By contrast, because I am habitually anxious, I tend to arrive early for trains and appointments, and my 'waiting' is fraught with frustration and impatience.

If I were more able to live light-heartedly and peacefully in the present moment—which, I maintain, includes awareness of the one before and the one after—perhaps there would be more of preparation in the truest, deepest sense. Not just trying-to-get-things-done-before-Christmas, but quietly watching as one does for the dawn; including notice of the streaks of light appearing in the sky and the first squawks of early birds.

Habitual watchers are alert to the surprising delights of life: situations and people—even ourselves—change for the better against all eventualities; and it is important to observe and be grateful that these things happen and may do so again. This relates to hope, which is surely something more than trusting all will be well, that things will turn out all right. For believing in the Gospel means putting one's whole trust in a Person rather than merely assenting to credal statements.

AUSTIN FARRER said, in a sermon preached at Trinity College, Oxford, that the manger had opened a scene of the 'powerlessness' of infancy which was crowned by the cross in the powerlessness of defeat, and the unconscious agony of birth by the conscious agony of dying.

The Incarnation, then, does not 'make everything all right' so that we can be carefree and carry on with life as we would wish to live it. God shares our human lot in order that we can proclaim with confidence the triumphant conclusion of the eighth chapter of St Paul's Epistle to the Romans:

> '... neither death, nor life, nor angels, nor principalities, nor things present, nor things to come, nor powers, nor height, nor depth, nor anything else in all creation, will be able to separate us from the love of God in Christ Jesus, our Lord.'

NATIVITY

THE MESSIAH whose coming was prophesied in the Old Testament and who is recognized by Christians in Jesus, is humble, gentle, and also slightly ridiculous.

Because we believe that God was 'silly in the crib' at Nazareth, as John Saward writes in his book Perfect Fools, Jesus is, has been, and always will be humanly present with every being. We can affirm this for others and for ourselves in our thought and prayer, certainly, but also in some measure practically by learning to cherish each successive present moment as the meeting point of time and eternity where mortal and immortal converge.

The image of Christ as Clown, which was revived some years ago in *Godspell*, is appropriate because the clown is one who plays a tragic role without ever taking himself or life too seriously. A good example for us, he can laugh at himself because he is devoid of conceit and self-importance and radiates what has been well described as a 'child-like, unmalicious, frolicsome quality'.

Humour is near to holiness, and love to laughter. That is why seemingly desperate situations in personal relationships or international affairs—for world politics depend ultimately on encounters between individuals—can often be resolved if the people concerned can simply smile at each other.

AT CHRISTMAS TIME we think especially of the Incarnation in respect of the ineffable God being of us and with us. Perhaps we should follow this thought to an enduring realization of the infinite potential and impenetrable mystery of every one of our fellow human beings.

Jesus teaches us to look at each individual person as unique and to consider the particular circumstances of every case in which a decision has to be made. This is not easy, but each of us can try in the limited sphere of our little lives not be pressurized into mass thinking. Instead, we need to remember the friendly greetings, the words of encouragement and sympathy, the small acts of kindness which people exchange a thousand times a day, and most of all in times of trouble, and which are the true measure of the spirit of mankind.

ONE OF THE MOST poignant moments in the Community's celebration of the Nativity is the singing of Laurence Housman's carol, 'The Maker of the Sun and Moon', after First Vespers. The newly decorated tree with its twinkling lights is in chapel and the bustle of preparation has hushed to quiet expectancy. So we come to the last verse:

'O perfect Love, outpassing sight
O Light beyond our ken,
Come down through all the world tonight
And heal the hearts of men.'

This urgent plea for help from God on behalf of his distracted and torn humankind is surely also a triumphant affirmation of what already *is*, that 'glimpse of all things gathered ... into Love'. We can pray that prayer only because our God is in fact the Love who has become incarnate in the utterly human man, Jesus Christ. So, as we look at God's world, we must pray in whatever way is proper to each of us, 'Lord have mercy'. We must also be profoundly thankful that he is in that world and that there is no situation of chaos, anguish, and horror from which God is absent: that, indeed, all things *are* gathered into Love.

THE PASSION

LENT, called 'this joyful season' in the first Lenten Preface of the Roman Missal, is essentially a spiritual springtime at the end of which we do not just thankfully abandon disciplines undertaken for its duration, but hope to go on into the rest of the Christian year walking more humbly and more wholly with God than we did before.

We cannot escape the fact that the victory of Easter is won on Good Friday. The risen life we live with Christ must, if it is real, witness to the ultimate transfiguration of evil and suffering through his sacrificial self-giving love.

Many of us pray 'may we be strangers no longer but pilgrims together on the way to your Kingdom'. It is certainly through our lives in families and in our church communities, as well as in the corporate life of the SLG convent, that we learn about our relationship to God.

As we all grow more aware of the precarious position of planet Earth, we realize our bondedness to each other—perhaps more acutely through what we share of the 'worst' rather than the 'best'. In any case, we cannot escape our interdependence both outward and inward. And what one does or suffers sooner or later affects all.

If Christians are to grasp anew something of God's good news, it will be in the context of belonging to the human lump. If we learn something more about experiencing here and now the dimensions of life eternal (not everlasting: it is about quality, not quantity) it will be through relationships with other people as well as with God.

People are real at a level deeper and more durable than anything we are able to perceive.

Lᴇɴᴛ ɪs ᴀ sᴇᴀsᴏɴ in which to recognize and acknowledge the great gulf between what we are and what God would have us be. How seriously do any of us ponder Christ's teaching set out in the Gospels of St Matthew (Chapters 5 to 7) and St Luke (Chapter 6)? Often it seems quite hopeless to try to apply this teaching in our twentieth-century lives, so intermeshed as they are with values that completely contradict it.

There is also the ever-present danger of striving to be what we would like ourselves to be and congratulating ourselves on any apparent success; or of ordering our actions primarily through fear, which Jeremy Taylor claims is the beginning of attrition, whereas 'contrition hath hope and love in it'.

By the time we come to Holy Week, we should hope to have cut loose from all these complexities and to be looking not at ourselves but towards God. Self-centred fear, attrition, is—as Jeremy Taylor says—'a good beginning but no more'. No doubt it is at least a start to recognize our deviousness, but we must not get stuck there, or too much concerned with our inability to improve ourselves. We have to reach out beyond, and in spite of, our sinfulness, in the hope and love which transcends fear.

RENASCENCE

PASSIONTIDE and Easter, in the rhythm of the Church's year, remind us annually of the tremendous truth of redemption. Perhaps each time we live through these seasons we see a little more clearly how impossible it is for creation to save itself, and how inexorable is the claim of the love that has saved, and goes on, saving us.

'Contrition hath hope and love in it'. Response to God's love requires genuine desire to relate to him as a person, and confidence that he gives us the grace to do so. He knows better than we do what wretched sinners we are, so we do not have to go on telling him. He knows that we owe everything to him, and he wants from us not grovelling gratitude but life-long companionship.

If we take seriously one particular aspect of the complex parable of the Prodigal Son, we can recognize God's humility in that of the forgiving father. He will not let his erring offspring have merely what he wishes or what he deserves, but sets him by his side to enjoy his company.

God is the supremely good companion, and to share our lives with him, 'we need not', as the hymn says, 'bid for cloistered cell/Our neighbour and our work farewell', but simply know that he is interestedly with us in every aspect of our lives.

THE MESSAGE of Easter opens up afresh for us each year the possibility of understanding more about what it means to be human in the light of the resurrection of Christ, and radically reverses our built-in assumption that death is the great and ultimate divider.

Few people would be greatly cheered if they believed that what the Church is about at this season is no more than the possibility of not dying 'indefinitely'. So perhaps it would be good if at Easter each one of us should seek out and articulate very simply what we really do believe about Easter and its consequences for ourselves in our own particular circumstances. Perhaps it is time to take seriously what Scripture, liturgy, and tradition tell us, that we take to heart in our everyday lives the true meaning of the message in the death and resurrection of God in Jesus Christ.

THE TRINITY, as has been said by Jürgen Moltmann, is no closed and self-sufficient circle, but an eschatalogical event, open to the future and containing the whole world with the miseries, sin, and goodness of all time.

We are drawn into God's perpetual movement of self-giving as it is depicted in Rublev's icon of the Trinity, and that is the eternal Easter experience which the Church celebrates.

THE SPIRIT of the resurrection reminds us that the Elder Son spent his Lent in isolation and self-satisfaction, but the contrition of the Prodigal brought *him* home to God.

When we consent to go out from what is safe and familiar to meet what is new and mysterious, we remove something of what blocks the way between our hearts and God. Year after year, Easter reminds us that God enables us to deepen our perception of the paschal mysteries at the heart of the Christian life.

In Oxford, daffodils are often in bloom on Ash Wednesday. As Isaiah says, 'The wilderness and the solitary place shall be glad for them; and the desert shall rejoice and blossom as the rose.'

CANDLES play an important part in our SLG life, and always their symbolic significance is linked with that of the paschal candle.

Each year, during the Easter Vigil, the paschal candle is lit from the new fire as we begin to celebrate the resurrection. 'Accept this Easter candle,' we pray, 'May it always dispel the darkness of this night!'

Easter is the annual reminder to Christians to affirm in our thinking and living the mighty truths of redemption and resurrection. The massive despair-provoking disasters, the evidence of our human greed and violence about which we are rightly concerned, are not the last word.

God's Kingdom *is* coming, through the small personal choices for God made by insignificant individuals, known to him alone. As the *Exultet* proclaims:

'May the Morning Star which never sets find this flame still burning: Christ, that Morning Star, who came back from the dead, and shed his peaceful light on all mankind, your Son who lives and reigns ... FOR EVER AND EVER.'

The Light of Christ shines in the darkness which cannot overcome it.

EPILOGUE

'...and the Word was made flesh.'

CHRISTMAS stands for something far beyond our comprehension and control. By taking humanity God has not, as it were, sanctioned our living life the way we'd like to, and given assurance that all will be well afterwards. What has happened is that God has shared historically in time, and is sharing now in the dimension of eternity, our human situation.

Jesus was hungry, thirsty, tired, according to the Gospels. Presumably he was also sometimes irritated and impatient; found life as untidy and full of dilemmas as we do; had to make, not clear-cut decisions between black and white, but bewildering ones between different, or sometimes identical, shades of grey. Probably he made mistakes and wrong judgements—though who is to say, in most cases, what ultimately proves to be 'wrong'? Surely, we cannot claim that the sinless Jesus had a complacent sense of his own virtue, for St Paul says he was 'made to be sin', which seems to imply an experience of the self-disgust and hopelessness which most of us know at some time or another.

All through this typically human experience, Jesus lived in a spirit of self-giving love towards God and man which brought on him the death through which sin and evil have been finally conquered. The 'hard and bitter agony' which the Incarnation means for us, is to choose in our own lives to live in the same spirit of self-giving love which, though it cuts across our natural inclinations, is possible because we belong to him.

The ultimate purpose of we Christians—Christ's Body, the Church—is not to live in hearty fellowship, doing good to others. It is so to have in and amongst us the mind of Christ, the spirit of his sacrificial love, that as we live, profoundly sharing and caring in the world, we meet the assaults and effects of evil from whatever source, inside or outside ourselves, as he did: open, vulnerable, and loving on the Cross.

> *'What his word doth make it*
> *That I believe and take it.'*

So said Queen Elizabeth I of the Eucharist; and each year, of course, the message of Christmas is essentially not what it means to me but the mighty act of redemption worked by God:

> 'That your faith might not rest in the wisdom of men
> but in the power of God.' (1 Cor. 2:5)